BEARDED DRAGONS

by Tom Mazorlig

INTRODUCING BEARDED DRAGONS

Technically speaking, the term "bearded dragon" can be applied to several species, all residing in the taxonomic genus *Pogona*. However, when most hobbyists use the term, they are referring to *Pogona vitticeps*, the Inland or Central Bearded Dragon. Within a few short years, the Inland Bearded Dragon has become one of the most frequently kept and bred of all the lizards. This is the only member of the genus that is firmly established in U.S. herpetoculture, though two others are available in small numbers.

Pogona is placed in the family Agamidae, which are roughly the Old World equivalents of American iguanids. This giant family includes the bearded dragons, the water dragons (*Physignathus*), the spiny-tails (*Uromastyx*), and a great number of other lizards. The genus *Pogona* is restricted to Australia, with one species or another being found almost everywhere on the continent. It contains roughly eight species of smallish to mid-sized lizards. They resemble the swifts and spiny lizards of North

T.F.H. Publications, Inc.
One TFH Plaza
Third and Union Avenues
Neptune City, NJ 07753

ISBN 0-7938-3020-6

CONTENTS

BEARDED DRAGONS

Despite their spiny appearance, most bearded dragons are docile animals, making good pet lizards for experienced keepers and first-timers alike. Photo by R. D. Bartlett.

America, filling approximately the same niche in the Australian deserts, scrubs, savannas, and open forests. These lizards range from being insectivores to omnivores. They are fast, efficient predators, and several species are semi-arboreal. *P. vitticeps* shares a small part of the southern end of its range with *P. barbata*, and overlaps in Queensland with *P. brevis*. The ranges of some of the western species also are somewhat overlapping.

THE THREE IMPORTANT DRAGONS

Pogona vitticeps, the Inland Bearded Dragon, is the common species in the hobby and the main subject of this book. Throughout the text, the term "bearded dragon" will be synonymous with "Inland Bearded Dragon." Out of the three beardies in the hobby, this is the only one the average hobbyist is likely to come across. This animal has become a mainstay of pet stores and hobbyist breeders. They are hardy and charming animals, completely deserving of their great popularity.

Two other species of *Pogona* are available, though they are not nearly so common as *P. vitticeps*. In fact, they can be very difficult to find. One of these is Rankin's Dragon (formerly called Lawson's Dragon). The scientific name of this species is in question. Hobbyists are currently using *Pogona brevis*, but it also has been called *Pogona rankini* and *Pogona henrylawsoni*. No matter the name used, this a nice little lizard. They are smaller than the Inland

Bearded Dragon, normally not being longer than 12 or 13 inches at most. In this species, the females and males tend to be more or less of equal size. Rankin's Dragon lacks the inflatable beard that most people associate with this genus. The popularity of Rankin's Dragon seems to be on the increase, as I have seen it at more reptile shows recently than in the past. In nature, they are found in central and western Queensland, overlapping the range of *P. vitticeps* and perhaps that of *P. barbata*.

The other bearded dragon in the hobby is the Eastern or Coastal Bearded Dragon, *Pogona barbata*. This species is roughly the same size as the Inland Bearded Dragon and somewhat darker and more drab in color. It nor-

Rankin's Dragon stays smaller than the Inland Bearded Dragon and makes a better choice for those keepers who are short on space. Photo by A. Both.

BEARDED DRAGONS

mally does not tame down as well as the other two species. It is the most resistant species to both cold and high humidity, as it ranges on the eastern and southeastern coast of Australia. The range includes the coasts of Queensland and New South Wales, northern Victoria, and the southern coast of South Australia. Coastal Bearded Dragons have the most impressive and energetic display of the three species. Although it once was the most common of the

bearded dragons in the hobby, it has become a species that is seen only rarely in the US.

THE COMMON DRAGON

As has been stated, when hobbyists use the phrase "bearded dragon," they are normally referring to the Inland Bearded Dragon. This animal has become a regular offer in pet stores and at herp shows. The reasons for this are the docile temperament, hardiness, and incredible fecundity of *P. vitticeps*.

The Inland Bearded Dragon is aptly named, as it is found in Australia's semi-arid interior, only reaching the coast in the southernmost part of its range. Their range could generally be described as the eastern part of central Australia. This includes parts of Queensland, New South Wales, Victoria, South Australia, and the Northern Territory.

The Inland Bearded Dragon is a mid-sized pet lizard, meaning smaller than a Giant Green Iguana but bigger than a Leopard Gecko. Males may be up to or slightly over two feet long, while females generally top out at 18 to 20 inches. About half of the total length of a bearded dragon is its tail. They are wide and bulky for their size. The bordering spines of the body and at the back of the head give them a resemblance to the horned lizards (genus *Phrynosoma*) of North and Central America. Bearded dragons have a very rough texture with the scales on the tail being keeled. With the beard blackened and inflated and the body puffed up with air, they look much more spiny then they actually are. The spines are rather flexible, but when the dragon is inflated, they are a bit sharp. In captivity, bearded dragons have a lifespan of approximately 7 to 12 years.

WILD DRAGONS

Bearded dragons are habitat generalists. They utilize desert, scrub, savanna, and semi-arid forests. When trees are available, they are semi-arboreal, but they will also perch on rocky outcroppings. They use these

Although once the most common of the bearded dragons in the hobby, the Coastal Bearded Dragon is now only available from specialist breeders. Photo by K. H. Switak.

The Inland Bearded Dragon normally has a pair of distinct spots at the base of the neck. These spots are not as apparent on the other species in the hobby. Photo by M. Walls.

establish territories, and breed. Remember that the seasons in the Southern Hemisphere are opposite those in the Northern Hemisphere. This means that the beardies are hibernating in July and August, emerging in September and October, and breeding in November and December. Left to their own devices, bearded dragons in the terrarium often stick to this breeding schedule, although hobbyists can manipulate conditions to get his or her dragons to breed at any time of the year.

The number and arrangement of the rows of lateral spines are important characters in bearded dragon identification. Photo by I. Francais.

high perches for basking, declaring dominance, and watching for predators and prey. At night and during inclement weather, bearded dragons will bury themselves in the dirt or, less often, hide under rocks, logs, or other debris. Adapted to life in areas of high heat, bearded dragons bask for much of the day, soaking up the heat and light of the sun. They are known to use sun-warmed surfaces, such as rocks and roads, to further keep their body temperatures high. *P. vitticeps* and *P. barbata* do well in moderately disturbed habitat and in some areas have become backyard lizards. They will bask on fences, mailboxes, and picnic tables when trees and rocks are scarce.

Depending on the severity of the winter, bearded dragons may dig a burrow and become torpid for the season or may just hide out during the worst of the weather. During the winter months, their food intake will drop and may cease all together, again depending on the severity of the winter in the given area. When spring rolls back around, they feed heavily,

Bearded dragons are opportunistic feeders showing little in the way of food preferences. The species in the hobby are all omnivores in the wild, the adults eating more plant matter than the juveniles. Just how much of the natural diet is vegetation remains uncertain, but a recent study suggested that *P. vitticeps* may lean towards complete herbivory as adults. I suspect that the components of the diet vary according to habitat, season, availability, and individual preference. Arthropods, other invertebrates, mammals, birds, and

Another important structure in *Pogona* taxonomy is the group of roughened scales at the base of the tail. The number, size, and arrangement of these scales provide clues for species identification. Photo by M. Walls.

The recent trend in the herp hobby is to selectively breed reptiles for specific colors and patterns. This process has begun to produce some attractive beardies like this gold phase male. Photo by R. Hunziker, courtesy of the Reptile Connection.

BEARDED DRAGONS

A bearded dragon's roughened skin provides many benefits in its natural habitat, possibly including camouflage, fearsome appearance, and reduced dehydration. Photo by M. Walls.

turn, bearded dragons serve as food for other creatures. Monitors, pythons, and other snakes and lizards will consume bearded dragons if they can. Bearded dragons are also preyed upon by dingoes, birds of prey, native cats and the introduced cats and dogs. Introduced rats will eat their eggs, as will several of the monitors. Hatchlings even may fall prey to funnel-web spiders, other large spiders, and large scorpions.

reptiles are consumed if they can be caught and subdued. Bearded dragons are not above eating smaller bearded dragons. They have been known to eat carrion on rare occasions. All forms and all parts of plants are eaten. In

This Coastal Bearded Dragon is engaged in a full display of his beard, greatly increasing the apparent size of his head and giving him a more fearsome appearance, hopefully scaring off rivals and predators. Photo by S. Minton.

BEHAVIOR

Bearded dragons exhibit many interesting and sometimes amusing behaviors in the wild and in the terrarium. Most of these are connected to territorial and breeding displays.

The most famous behavior of bearded dragons is undoubtedly the inflation of their beards. What we call a beard is actually an expandable pouch of skin in the gular area. The scales in this area are large and come to fine points. When upset or excited, a dragon fills the pouch with air. The pouch greatly expands in volume, and the pointed spines stick out. The color of the beard rapidly darkens. This all gives the illusion that the dragon has gotten larger and spinier. The males in particular have very well-developed beards, and those of the males tend to be very black when expanded. Combined with a gaping, yellow mouth and some hissing, the beard makes a

In social situations, the dominant bearded dragon, usually a male, will occupy the highest perch available. From such a spot, the lizard has the best view of approaching rivals. Photo by I. Francais.

rather convincing threat. Inflating the beard occurs in response to a perceived threat from a predator, as part of the territorial defense of the males, and during courtship. When threatened or confronted with a rival, the beard is inflated, the mouth opened, and the body elevated high on the toes. The tail is lashed at the opponent, and biting is sure to follow if these threats are not heeded.

Another behavior used in both defense and courtship is head-bobbing. This behavior is almost exclusively performed by the males as a way of proclaiming dominion and advertising their virility. Generally, they stand high up on their toes, darken their throats, and vigorously nod their heads up and down. Most often, this behavior is performed on a conspicuous limb or rock. Other males in the region will respond in kind, and, if one ventures too close to another, the head-bobbing will get more energetic until a true territorial skirmish erupts.

One of the more strange and amusing behaviors executed by beardies is arm-waving. This is an appeasement gesture performed by subordinate bearded dragons when confronted by a dominant one. The lizard stands on three feet while waving one of the forelegs in a slow circle. I think it looks as though the little lizards are performing some form of reptilian semaphore. Arm-waving is performed by juveniles, females, and subordinate males. It generally keeps aggressive males from attacking them. It is also used by nonreceptive females to ward off males intent on courting them. In a cage of hatchlings, one dragon arm-waving can start the whole group doing it, a very funny sight.

BEARDED DRAGONS

In a bearded dragon cage perhaps it is best to use artificial plants, as these will withstand crushing and nibbling better than real ones. Photo by I. Francais.

THE ENCLOSURE

Before bringing home a bouncing bearded dragon, it is wise to have an enclosure ready. This will give you somewhere warm and cozy to put your new friend immediately, instead of having him sit in a box while you scramble around assembling equipment. This will greatly reduce the stress factor for your beardie. Once you have him in the cage, leave him alone for a day or so, giving him a chance to adjust to his new surroundings. Bearded dragons are hardy and durable animals, but you still want to cause them as little stress as possible. They usually will be willing to eat during their first day home, but you should not be worried if your new pet refuses food for a day or two after the big move.

A DRAGON'S LAIR

There are many types of enclosures that can be used to house bearded dragons. Glass aquaria used for fish perhaps are the most commonly used dragon pens. The advantages to using glass aquaria are several. They are readily available, not too expensive, easy to clean, and easy to heat. For one or even a pair of bearded dragons, a fish tank will make a satisfactory home.

If you are housing a small colony or want something spacious for your pair or individual, you should probably not use an aquarium.

The aquarium large enough for a small breeding group would be extremely heavy and expensive. Also, since fish tanks only open from the top, cleaning would be difficult.

One option would be to buy a molded plastic cage. There are several brands available at herp shows and through catalogs. These usually have sliding front doors to facilitate cleaning and vents in the top for lighting. While these cages are expensive (especially for one large enough to house some beardies), they are durable, attractive, easy to clean, light-weight, and easy to heat.

Some keepers, especially those who want to house several breeding groups, use cattle watering troughs as their dragon pens. These are made of either heavy-duty plastic or aluminum. They are tall enough use without a lid, as long as there are no cats or other pets in the house that could climb in and snack on the beardies. You will also have to be careful that the climbing branches do not come too close to the top, allowing the dragons to leap out of the trough. Lights can easily be affixed to the rim or suspended from above for heating. Troughs are fairly easy to clean especially if you can take them outside and hose them down.

Custom-made cages are also popular with bearded dragon aficionados. Most often these are made of wood and wire. One-eighth inch gauge hardware cloth works very well; any size up to a half inch should be fine. However, any size larger than one-

Like the adults, hatchling bearded dragons love to climb and feel most secure when given a perch. Photo by M. Walls.

BEARDED DRAGONS

For ease of climbing and the lizard's comfort, branches and limbs in a bearded dragon enclosure should have a greater diameter than the body of the cage occupants. Photo by A. Norman.

eighth inch will allow crickets to escape. Chicken wire is too big, and it may allow dragons to get their heads caught. Custom-made cages are relatively inexpensive but may take considerable time and a small supply of tools to make.

When building a custom cage, make sure that you design it to be easily accessible for cleaning. The easier the cage is to clean, the more dutiful you probably will be in your cleaning chores. Also, easy access makes it more likely you will handle your beardie, which is important if you want a "dog-tame" pet. You will need to build it such that the lizards cannot burn themselves on heat lamps but will be able to get warm enough. Also, if using wire, be sure that there are not sharp ends hanging where the lizards can puncture themselves. If you get in touch with a herpetological society, you are sure to meet some people who have built their own cages and would be happy to share their ideas with you.

Here is a bearded dragon housed in well-landscaped enclosure. The rocks and wood are important for climbing and establishing a territory. Photo by W. P. Mara.

When housed together, bearded dragons often pile up on top of each other. The reason for this curious behavior is not known. Photo by I. Francais.

BEARDED DRAGONS

Size Matters

As has been mentioned, bearded dragons are largish and active lizards. This translates into a need for a lot of space. Additionally, they, especially males, can be fiercely territorial. So, within reason, the bigger the enclosure the better. While a juvenile may be fine in a 20-gallon long aquarium (30"l x 12"w x 10"h), an adult would be cramped and unhappy. For a single adult bearded dragon, you should allow roughly 36"l x 18"w x 16"h, which is the size of a standard 40-gallon breeder aquarium. A pair needs at least 72"l x 18"w x 16"h, or a 125-gallon aquarium. Remember that these should be considered bare minimum sizes, and larger cages would even be

better. In all of the above examples, more vertical space would be beneficial. Bearded dragons love to climb, and the vertical space allows them more options for thermoregulation.

Decor

There are many options for outfitting a bearded dragon cage. You could design a stunning, naturalistic habitat or go with something simple and functional. No matter what decorative ideas you have, the primary consideration must remain the needs of the animals living in the enclosure.

There are many substrates that will be adequate for a bearded dragon enclosure. Which one you choose will depend upon availabil-

ity, budget, and preference. For a bare-bones, functional cage, newspaper is fine. It is far from attractive, but it is readily available. Additionally, it is cheap (even free), absorbent, and easy to clean. Newspaper must be replaced frequently. Processed recycled newspaper beddings are growing in popularity. These can be expensive and drab-looking but otherwise make a superior bedding. They readily absorb wastes, making them easy to clean. Usually, you will not have to replace it all, instead scooping out the soiled area. It is a soft bedding that allows for the natural burrowing behavior of bearded dragons. Supposedly, if swallowed by your lizard, the processed newspaper will

Many keepers house their bearded dragons on sand. The red sand sets off the pattern of this Rankin's Dragon very well. Photo by A. Both.

pass through the digestive tract without causing any ill effects.

If you want to go with a more natural look for your cage, sand makes an excellent choice. There are now sands made for use in reptile enclosures. These should not cause problems if swallowed, and there are several colors available. Sand holds heat very well. Wastes dry out quickly and then easily can be scooped out. If you put several inches in the cage, the dragons will burrow down into it. Sand can get very heavy, so be sure that whatever the enclosure rests upon can withstand the weight.

Although bearded dragons are not skittish animals, they will appreciate a hide box. Often, they will retreat into the box at night. Place the hide box somewhere in between the warm and cool ends of the cage, or put one at each end. This way, the animals will not have to choose between security and a preferred temperature. There are several options for hide boxes. There are attractive, naturalistic ceramic ones available at most pet stores. Large rounds of cork bark are simple and attractive. Cardboard boxes can be used and are easy to replace. If the substrate is very deep, the beardies may burrow under it instead of using a box. Many keepers do not include a hide box in their dragon enclosures; it is not a strict necessity. If you elect to include hide boxes in your enclosure, there should be at the very least one per dragon plus one.

Bearded dragons love to climb. Some individuals will spend most of the day

Bearded dragons greatly resemble the North American swifts of the genus *Sceloporus* in body structure and habits. Photo by J. Merli.

perched high on a limb surveying their domain. You should place some limbs, branches, rocks, and other climbing materials in the enclosure to enable your dragons to climb. You will have to make sure that these are secured in place so that the beardies cannot dislodge them and injure themselves. A nontoxic epoxy will do the job. Ideally, the perches will be about the same diameter as the body of the beardie. Rough surfaces, such as

natural branches, are easier for the beardies to climb on than smoother surfaces. Most pet stores sell a variety of wood, rocks, and artificial alternatives. Many keepers use wood and rocks from outdoors. This is fine, but precautions must be taken to avoid introducing diseases and parasites to your pets. The best way to avoid such a disaster is to soak materials from outdoors in a fairly strong solution of bleach and water (and it would do no

Bearded dragons are good subjects for large desert terraria. Such elaborate enclosures will require a lot of maintenance but will make a stunning addition to any room. Photo by A. Both.

BEARDED DRAGONS

When cold, a bearded dragon will flatten out and angle its body to present as much surface area as possible to the warm rays of the sun (or the heat lamp). Photo by U. E. Friese.

harm to sterilize store-bought cage fixtures the same way) for at least 20 minutes; this should kill next to all the pathogens that could be present. After this, rinse the materials **thoroughly** in plain water to remove the bleach. Be careful about this, as the fumes from bleach can cause your pets serious distress. Allow the objects to dry out before placing them in the cage. If you want to use driftwood from the ocean, soak it in several changes of fresh water to remove the salt before bleaching it.

Lastly, remember that bearded dragons have a high metabolism, meaning they produce lots of waste. You should scoop out the waste on a daily basis and completely clean the cage and all fixtures at least once a month. Use a weak bleach solution to disinfect it. Completely replace the substrate, also.

HEATING AND LIGHTING

Some Like it Hot

Bearded dragons originate in the hot, dry interior of Australia. They are given to prolonged spells of basking beneath the blazing sun. When they reach their preferred temperature, they move out of the sun, beneath a log or rock or under the sand. After cooling down they move back out into the sun, and so on. Regulating body temperature through behavior is called behavioral thermoregulation. Nearly all reptiles and amphibians control their body temperature this way.

Bearded dragons have adapted to the intense heat of the Australian desert; they are rather resistant to overheating. Also, due to the great differences in daytime and nighttime temperatures, beardies can withstand (and may prefer) wide fluctuations in temperature over the course of a day.

Bearded dragons in captivity must be given access to high temperatures like those found in their natural environment. But, providing intense heat is not enough. You must set up the cage in such a way that the lizards can regulate their own temperatures. This is not as difficult as it sounds, particularly in a large enclosure. In brief, if all the heating equipment is at one end of the cage, the other end will be substantially cooler, and the lizards can move between the two ends to control their internal temperature.

In more detail, you will want to set up all the basking and warming areas at one end of the enclosure. Since bearded dragons are a heliophilic (sun-loving) species that thermoregulates using direct sunlight in the wild, the best way to heat them is by the use of incandescent light bulbs. The wattage and number of bulbs you will need to use depends on the size of the cage and the number of beardies you are housing in it. As a general guideline, a 100-watt bulb is sufficient for a 30-gallon aquarium, but,

depending on the ambient temperature of your house, this could be too little or too much heat. Also, glass aquaria will hold heat better than a wood and wire cage.

The only way to be sure that you are providing a proper range of temperatures is to use a thermometer. Pet stores will carry a number of different designs of thermometer. The digital ones that can store the highest and lowest temperatures in a 24-hour period (called min/max thermometers) are probably the best kind as they allow close monitoring of the temperature even when you are not actually present. For bearded dragons, the cool end of the cage should be around 75°F (24°C) and the warm end

Hatchlings are somewhat more sensitive to extreme temperatures than the adults. Photo by J. Prime.

Having a flattened rock or piece of wood beneath the basking light will give your beardie a nice warm surface to bask on. Test the spot with a thermometer to make sure it is not too hot. Photo by I. Francais.

BEARDED DRAGONS

near 90-95°F (32-35°C). They also should have a basking spot that runs 105°F (41°C) or even a little higher. At night, the temperature in the cage can safely drop down into the mid-sixties (roughly 17-18°C).

To make these warmer basking spots, angle a wide branch up toward the light. Make sure that the lizards cannot come into contact with the bulb. Most reptiles, bearded dragons included, actually will press against light bulbs if given the chance and burn themselves. Sometimes the burns are bad enough to be fatal. Remember that bearded dragons are territorial lizards. The largest, most aggressive individual will attempt to monopolize the basking spot. Therefore, you should include at least one basking perch per dragon, and having an extra will not hurt.

Hot rocks will not significantly contribute to the warmth in the cage. Lizards will tend to sit for long periods of time on hot rocks, possibly getting burned. Therefore, their use is not recommended. If you need some additional heat, it is better to use heat tape, an undertank heater, or a pig blanket. Undertank heaters are safe and easy to use but are designed to attach to the bottom of glass aquaria. If you have some other type of cage, you must consider one of the other options, which will require more knowledge and care to install. If in doubt, consult an electrician rather than risk a house fire. Lastly, ceramic heat emitters provide heat from above without giving off light, making them ideal for nighttime heating. Heat emitters must be housed in ceramic fixtures but otherwise can be treated like normal lightbulbs.

Here Comes the Sun

Aside from warmth and photoperiod, the sun provides bearded dragons and other heliophilic animals (including humans) with another commodity: vitamin D. The ultraviolet-B waves (UV-B) produced by the sun provide the energy for the formation of the active form of the vitamin. This takes place in the skin through a complex biochemical process. Vitamin D is necessary for the normal metabolism of calcium and phosphorus; without it, skeletal abnormalities develop.

Although it is believed that bearded dragons can obtain adequate amounts of vitamin D from a rich and balanced diet, most keepers also provide full-spectrum lighting so their pets can make their own metabolically. Full-spectrum lights are fluorescent tubes designed to be mimics of natural sunlight. Although they are not very similar, full-spectrum lights are the best

The hot and dry conditions of the Australian desert must be duplicated in the terrarium if you expect your bearded dragon to thrive. This is a wild individual. Photo by K. H. Switak.

substitute humans have yet invented. They provide UV-A and UV-B. UV-A rays are thought to regulate natural behaviors, including foraging and reproduction. There is even evidence that some lizard species can see UV-A rays; some keepers and herpetologists believe UV-A helps make food appear more appealing.

Recently, there has been some controversy about full-spectrum lights. While no one is saying they harm animals, some keepers are saying that they do not provide any benefits to animals. There is still a lot of research to be done, and the available lights could use improving, but I swear by them in my own collections. I'm convinced the installation of such a light

reversed metabolic bone disease in my iguana. Admittedly, some keepers never use full-spectrum lighting with any of their herps and don't have problems with metabolic

bone disease. In short, no one definitely knows how necessary or unnecessary full-spectrum lighting is.

I believe it is best to include full-spectrum lighting in the

Bearded dragons are semi-social. Given enough space, several can be kept in the same cage, provided there is only one male in the group. Photo by R. D. Bartlett

BEARDED DRAGONS

In nature, some populations of bearded dragons show colors that match the sands and rocks of their location. Photo by Z. Takacs.

BEARDED DRAGONS

Housing your beardies outdoors will provide them with plenty of natural sunlight and a wide variety of food. However, building a suitable enclosure can be an expensive undertaking. Photo by U. E. Friese.

housing of bearded dragons. These are animals that bask heavily in nature. They would be exposed to very high amounts of ultra-violet light. So, no harm can come from the much lower levels of UV light that full-spectrum lighting will produce. In using full-spectrum lighting, three things are important. First, choose a bulb that is for reptiles specifically. Plant bulbs and ones made for human seasonal affective disorder generally do not provide enough UV-B for lizards. Secondly, the ability to produce UV-B fails before the light will. Generally, you should replace your bulbs once or twice yearly. Follow the manufacturer's guidelines on how often to replace the bulb. Lastly, the light must be close enough to your pet without intervening filters. Glass and plexiglass both filter out UV light. Screen will, also, but to a much lesser extent. The UV-B produced by full-spectrum bulbs only penetrates to a distance of 10-12 inches. Your beardies must be able to get that close to the bulb without actually contacting it. The easiest way to do that is to position the light over the highest basking site in the cage. Remember that beardies will compete for basking space, so you may have to include several sites if you are housing a group.

Photoperiod is an important but somewhat overlooked aspect of herp husbandry. In natural surroundings, reptiles are exposed to definite periods of day and night, and the lengths of these periods vary with the seasons according to the latitudes a given animal comes from. Bearded dragons will do well with a photoperiod of 12 hours of day and 12 hours of night (normally expressed 12:12). If you wish to give your beardies a quasi-natural seasonal cycle, you can vary the photoperiod over the course of the year. In the summer, give them approximately a 14:10 ratio; in the winter reverse this to 10:14. In the fall and spring, the photoperiod will be 12:12. Make these changes gradually over the course of a week or so. Hooking the lights up to a timer will facilitate this process. An added bonus of manipulating the photoperiod is the increased chance of stimulating your beardies to breed.

OUTDOORS?

Yes, this is possible. If you live in a warm and relatively dry area, your beardies will thrive outdoors. Even if only the summers in your area are suitable, you can house your beardies outside for the season, bringing them inside when the weather becomes unfavorable. Remember that these are arid-dwelling lizards naturally. If your area is humid or damp, it will be best to keep your dragons indoors.

Deciding to move your beardies outdoors is not to be taken lightly. It is true that they will benefit from the natural sunlight, fresh air, and increased variety of insects; there are negative aspects as well. For one, you must be absolutely positive that the weather will not become so inclement as to endanger your lizards. Since this is next to impossible to do, you will have to provide shelters from severe weather and be prepared to move your lizards back inside.

You also will have to secure the enclosure against local predators. Many animals will not hesitate to add a bearded dragon to their diet. Some of these predators include (depending on your locality) raccoons, cats, dogs, coyotes, hawks, and snakes. A fenced-in yard will help dissuade human predators, as well. Lastly, there is a small danger that your lizards will pick up parasites from the soil or the wild insects they consume.

I'm not telling you all of this to dissuade you from housing

Newspaper is a suitable substrate for beardies. If you do use newspaper, provide your dragon with some hide boxes, as it will not be able to burrow under the paper to hide. Photo by I. Francais

your dragons outdoors; these are just things you will want to consider and prepare for. Keepers who house their dragons outdoors claim they are healthier and more robust than those housed solely indoors, but there is no hard evidence for this.

Building a permanent, outdoor enclosure will require a substantial investment of time and money. A number of tools and construction know-how are essential. Wood and heavy-duty screening are probably

the best materials for an outdoor cage. It is probably best to make the bottom of the enclosure walls solid both for structural stability and the protection of your beardies. Make the top half of the walls and the roof of screening to allow in beneficial sunlight.

If you use the ground for the bottom of the cage, your beardies can engage in natural burrowing and nesting behavior. To prevent them from burrowing out of the enclosure, you will need to

Many keepers use one of the several suitable beddings made of wood chips or shavings for their bearded dragons. Photo by W. P. Mara.

BEARDED DRAGONS

In the outdoor enclosure, you must be sure your dragons have shady areas to retreat to should they become too hot. Photo by U. E. Friese.

sink the walls into the ground to a depth of about 18 inches. Keep in mind the minimum dimensions suggested above, although, freed from the constraints of fitting the cage into your indoor living space, you should be able to make the enclosure quite large. You probably will want to make the enclosure tall enough for you to stand up. This will make cleaning much easier.

Include plenty of large wood and rock perches for basking and remember to have enough of these for the number of dragons you are keeping.

They will squabble over favored spots; the less dominant individuals will need to have spaces of their own. In a large enclosure, you can probably get away with having more than one male, but keep an eye out that territorial squabbles don't result in injuries.

The enclosure will look better with the inclusion of live plants. Taking into account the climate of your area, there should be several varieties that will be suitable. Because bearded dragons are omnivorous, they are likely to

nibble on the plants. Therefore, you must be certain these plants will be edible. They will also have to withstand the trampling these lizards will dish out. Snake plant, yucca, *Ficus*, hibiscus (and the closely related roses of sharon), juniper, and palms are suitable, and there are many other possibilities. Many herbs will grow in the dry, sunny conditions likely to exist in a dragon enclosure. Some to consider including are rosemary, sage, lavender, and thyme. All of these will do no harm to your dragons if they are ingested. Talk with the staff at your local nursery who will have many helpful suggestions.

The fixtures should be secured in place but be removable so that they may be cleaned thoroughly. Water containers can be as large as you like, but also must be removable. The water dishes may need to be cleaned daily. You should rake away the droppings on a regular basis and replace the top few inches of dirt every year. Instead of replacing it, you could completely turn the soil over to a depth of 6 to 8 inches. Be sure you don't unearth any eggs when you do this!

A final note on outdoor caging: you will have to keep a close eye on females when the time to lay eggs approaches. Once a female completes her nest it will be almost invisible. It is unlikely the eggs will incubate successfully outdoors, so you will need to be able to locate a nest and dig up the eggs. You should dig them up as soon as possible, or they might succumb to inclement weather or ants.

Large cattle watering troughs can be adapted to housing bearded dragons. If you have a garden hose, they are quite easy to clean. Photo by I. Francais.

Given the proper conditions, bearded dragons are very hardy animals that will provide their keepers with years of enjoyment. Photo by I. Francais.

DIET and HEALTH

You may want to consider using forceps when hand-feeding your dragon to avoid being accidentally bitten. Photo by I. Francais.

Wild bearded dragons take a wide variety of foods normally, including substantial quantities of vegetation. They are true omnivores, eagerly consuming all manner of insects, other invertebrates, small vertebrates, leaves, flowers, and fruits. A bearded dragon keeper must provide his/her charges with the varied and well-balanced diet they need.

THE MENU

It is useful for keepers to think of a bearded dragon's diet as being composed of two parts: animals (or prey, or meat, or whatever term you wish to use) and vegetables. By animals, I mean insects, arthropods, other invertebrates, and small vertebrates. Vegetables include leaves, fruits, flowers, and root parts.

Let's look at each of these components more closely

The vast majority of prey normally fed to beardies consists of insects. Bearded dragons are not fussy about what insects they eat. The general rule is "if it moves, eat it." Insects are fed live to beardies, who will chase them excitedly around the cage. You can catch food for your dragons yourself, but it will be very time consuming to catch the large quantities of bugs that even one bearded dragon will eat on a regular basis. Therefore, most keepers buy insects.

If you opt to catch food for your beardies, always be sure you take insects from areas that are free of pesticides, herbicides, etc. Public lands, especially in cities, are often sprayed with chemicals.

Check with your public works department if in doubt. You should also become familiar with the naturally noxious insect species that occur in your area (Monarch Butterflies and their larvae and lubber grasshoppers come to mind). Moths, june beetles, earthworms, grasshoppers, and flies will be eaten rapidly and provide some variety. My dragons seem to especially enjoy chasing moths and leap after them with gusto. Remember that when feeding wild-caught food, there is a minor risk of introducing parasites to your lizards. Keep an eye out for signs of infestations.

If you do not wish to catch food, live insects are available at most pet stores and are inexpensive. Crickets are the easiest to come by and are probably the best insect to

> Like many lizards, bearded dragons have a protusile and sticky tongue used to catch insect prey. Their tongue is not terribly long but is used with great effectiveness. Photo by I. Francais.

Waxworms are another suitable food item for bearded dragons. They should be vitamin dusted since they are hard to gut-load. Photo by M. Gilroy.

use as a staple food. Mealworms, waxworms, fruit flies, and occasionally other insects may also be available at your local store. If you keep a group of beardies, you will probably want to order insects in large quantities both to save money (crickets get much cheaper when ordered in thousand lots) and trips to and from a pet store.

A large portion of the nutritional content of insects resides in the undigested and partially digested food in their guts. Healthy, well-fed insects provide more nutrients to captive lizards than do starved ones. Many pet stores do not feed their feeder insects very well. Therefore, if you bring your crickets home from the pet store and immediately dump them into your beardie's cage, you have given your beardie little more than some carbohydrates, fats, and water. It is much better for your bearded dragon if you feed it crickets and other insects that are themselves fed a nutritious diet. Additionally, if you order insects in large quantities, feeding them a good diet will help keep them alive and healthy long enough to be fed to your beardie.

Crickets are one of the easiest of the commercially available insects to keep. A simple, escape-proof container with food and some hiding areas (a few layers of egg crates or crumpled pieces of newspaper will do nicely) is all they require. In my experience, having a substrate complicates cleaning and isn't worth the effort. Crickets generally will eat anything, so providing a nutritious diet for them (and, thus, for your beardies) is fairly easy. Wheat bran or whole-grain bread makes a good base. Along with that, provide some nutritious greens, like collards, mustard, or kale, and a few slices of some juicy fruit, like orange, apple, or squash, for moisture. Any other ends of fruits and vegetables you want to throw in will be consumed as well. There are also commercial cricket foods available that provide a nice, well-rounded, and convenient diet. Crickets are rather dirty animals; you will need to clean out the cricket cage frequently. Change the food at least every other day to avoid producing fruit flies and unpleasant odors.

Mealworms should be kept in a few inches of wheat bran or oatmeal with some slices of squash or sweet potato on top. Some leafy greens and their stems can be included for an extra nutrient boost. The vegetables must be

This is an appropriate setup for keeping a large number of crickets on hand for feeding beardies. Photo by I. Francais.

Giant mealworms can be used to add variety to the diet of adult bearded dragons. Beardies seem to enjoy changes in their diets. Photo by I. Francais.

changed daily, or mold will develop. King mealworms are probably the best variety to feed adult beardies, since they are sizable enough for a few to make a decent meal. Smaller varieties are useful for younger beardies. Bearded dragons are happy to eat the beetles the mealworms turn into as well.

Pinky mice make a very nutritious addition to the diet. Large juvenile and adult beardies can eat them without a problem. Photo by I. Francais.

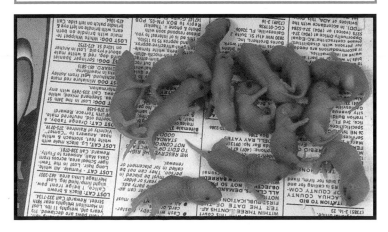

Waxworms are larval moths that live in beehives eating the wax and honey. Due to their specialized diet, it is difficult to keep them alive for very long. Instead, buy them in quantities you can feed out in a day or two and dust them in supplements before feeding. These are reported to be very high in fat so do not feed waxworms to your dragons too often.

In addition to the normal feeding of the feeder insects, it is recommended that you pack your feeder insects with high amounts of vitamins and minerals on a regular basis. This process is commonly called "gut-loading" in the hobby. Crickets are easy to gut-load. The day before you

BEARDED DRAGONS

Parsley is rich in vitamin A, vitamin C, calcium, and other nutrients. Both the flat and curly varieties make good food for beardies. Photo by M. Walls.

Kale is rich in many nutrients and available in most grocery stores. Photo by M. Walls.

are going to feed a group of crickets to your beardies, separate them from the others. Put them in a small container with a slice of orange for moisture. Give them the regular food, but mix or coat the food heavily in a vitamin/mineral and calcium supplements. Allow them to feed on this for 12 to 24 hours before feeding to your bearded dragons. If you let the crickets feed on this mineral-rich food for much longer than this, most of them will die. The high mineral content will plug up the digestive tracts of the crickets. Gut-loading is good for all bearded dragons, but it is especially important to do with the food for breeding females and hatchlings.

Many keepers also feed mice to their bearded dragons. As long as the mice are healthy, there is no need to supplement them when they are being fed to bearded dragons. The dragons will obtain minerals and vitamins from the bones and other internal organs. Mice tend to be somewhat high in fat, so they should not be fed to beardies too often. However, some keepers exclusively feed mice to their adults without any visible problems. They feed their beardies less often to avoid making them obese. Mice will help keep weight on a breeding female and prevent her from using up her own mineral stores when making eggshells. Most bearded dragons will eat pre-killed mice, fresh or frozen and thawed, without a problem. If you decide to feed live mice, never leave a live mouse unattended in the cage with your lizard. Mice have been known to attack, injure, and even kill snakes and lizards if not eaten right away.

Vegetation is the second major component of a proper bearded dragon diet. Most of the items in the produce department of your local grocery store make good additions to the menu. The majority of the vegetables you feed should be highly nutritious, calcium-rich, leafy greens. Some excellent choices are collard greens, mustard greens, turnip tops, dandelions, parsley, and cilantro (also called coriander and Chinese parsley). Kale

This is a highly nutritious salad prepared for adult bearded dragons. For smaller ones, the pieces should be smaller and the hard vegetables grated. Photo by M. Walls.

This bearded dragon is eager to feed on his snack of moistened alfalfa pellets, monkey chow, peas, and carrots. Remember not to overfeed these voracious animals. Photo by I. Francais.

and cabbage-type vegetables (broccoli and Brussels sprouts) interfere with production of thyroid hormones, so these should be fed sparingly. Spinach and swiss chard contain chemicals which combine with calcium and prevent its absorption by the digestive tract. Again, feed these vegetables sparingly. Bearded dragons and other desert-dwelling lizards seem to enjoy pungent herbs. These will cause no harm if not fed in large quantities. (For the most part, herbs have many biologically active compounds, so feeding in large quantities can have bad results.) Some of the safest to feed are rosemary, oregano, basil, chives, sage, and marjoram.

Besides the leafy greens, many other fruits and vegetables can and should be included in the diet. These would include carrots (with tops), bell peppers, okra, squash, celery, corn, green beans, kiwis, grapes, bananas, raspberries, and papayas, to name but a few of the many items available. If you have access to a garden or orchard, the leaves of grapes, mulberries, apples, radishes, and roses will make for some nutritious variety in the diet. Colorful flowers seem to be favored by beardies. Roses, dandelions, hibiscus,

As beardies are adapted to arid conditions, they need access to a water bowl only two or three days each week. The bowl should be cleaned between each use. Photo by J. Balzarini.

day lilies, and lavender all make fine occasional treats. All vegetables should be grated, shredded, or chopped into bite-sized pieces. Frozen vegetables can be used, but always make sure they are thoroughly thawed out before feeding.

The majority of bearded dragon keepers probably feed their lizards mostly insects with some fruits and vegetables every now and then. However, recent research has suggested wild, adult bearded dragons may take up to 90% of their total food as vegetation, at least in certain habitats at certain times of the year. More research must be performed before we can say exactly what fraction of a bearded dragon's food should be vegetables.

With my own breeding colony, a fifty-fifty mix of animal and vegetable foodstuffs has worked very well at keeping my adults happy, healthy, and breeding. Hatchlings and juveniles should be fed a lower proportion of vegetation than the adults.

Supplements make up a small but critical portion of a complete bearded dragon diet. In addition to feeding the crickets and mealworms a good diet and gut-loading them, they should be coated in a vitamin supplement regularly. Coating feeder insects is very easy. Place the insects in a bag or jar with a small amount of the supplement. Gently shake the container for a few seconds or so. This is called "dusting"

and "shake'n'bake" by many hobbyists. All the insects should be liberally covered in the powder.

Always use vitamin and mineral supplements that are specifically formulated for reptiles and amphibians. They may be slightly more expensive than cat or dog vitamins, but they are definitely better for your dragon. Every reptile enthusiast probably has their own opinion on which vitamin and mineral supplements are best to use. I say that when you find one that seems to keep your animals healthy, growing, and breeding you should stick with it. There are some qualities you can look for in supplements to help you distinguish the best ones from the rest.

Hatchlings are somewhat touchy to feed. Be very careful that you feed them small crickets; generally two-week-old crickets will be the perfect size. Photo by I. Francais.

When housing bearded dragons together, monitor them at feeding time to make sure each one is getting adequate food. Photo by I. Francais.

BEARDED DRAGONS

Some of the better supplements contain beta carotene instead of vitamin A. Beta carotene is a plant-derived compound that is converted to vitamin A as needed by the body. This is important because vitamin A is toxic in high amounts. Since the lizard's body will only convert as much beta carotene into vitamin A as it needs, there is no danger of overdosing your pet.

The ratio of the amount of calcium to the amount of phosphorus in the supplement you choose should be 2:1 or greater. If the proportion of phosphorus is higher than this, it will interfere with the absorption of calcium, which will eventually lead to metabolic bone disease. It is thought that calcium will degrade some vitamins, so, if possible, buy separate vitamin and calcium supplements. Mixing them together when gut-loading or dusting will not allow enough time for the calcium to degrade the vita-

mins, so you do not need to be concerned about this. Some keepers even insist that there should be no minerals whatsoever mixed in with the vitamins, that both the vitamin supplement and the mineral supplement should be completely separate. I don't believe this is necessary, but I freely admit that the jury is still out on this question.

FEEDING REGIMEN

Bearded dragons are active lizards with a high metabolism. As such, they must be fed frequently. Most keepers feed their dragons daily or every other day. They will eat a lot of food at each feeding. Since the diet and frequency of feeding change slightly over the lifespan, I am presenting the diet arranged according to the age of the beardie in question. Remember that at all ages clean, fresh water should be available all the time (although most beardies seldom drink).

Hatchlings (up to four months old)

The main concern when feeding hatchlings is the size of the food offered. Hatchlings that consume insects that are too large often suffer from paralysis followed by death. It is **imperative** that you feed hatchling bearded dragons insects that are **one-third or less** the size of their head. Mealworms should be **completely excluded** from the diet until the hatchling is four months old or so. The hard, chitinous exoskeleton of mealworms causes much the same problems as feeding insects that are too large. Perhaps the ideal food for hatchlings is two-week-old crickets, often called "fly-sized" by hobbyists. If your local pet store doesn't carry this size of cricket normally, they may be willing to order them, especially if you are buying in quantity. House flies and fruit flies also make good victuals for hatchling beardies, but they are harder to feed and gut-load.

Hatchlings should be fed insects at least two times daily, making sure each lizard gets a few crickets; each should eat a much greater number of fruit flies in a feeding. If you do not feed a group of hatchlings with this frequency, they will begin to pick on one another, resulting in babies missing digits, limbs, and tails. In severe instances, a hatchling may be killed by its siblings. A wise breeder keeps his hatchlings well fed.

Once a day, the insects should be dusted in supplements. Offer vegetation frequently, grated and shredded into bite-sized pieces. If

Baby bearded dragons need to be fed a high quality diet in generous quantities to provide them with enough nutrients to fuel their rapid growth and development. Photo by I. Francais.

This bearded dragon has an obviously misshapen snout. This is most likely the result of rubbing his snout against the walls of his cage, a common behavior for lizards inadequately housed. Photo by J. Balzarini.

you are raising a group of bearded dragons together, you would be wise to feed some vegetables daily. With my own babies this has resulted in a much lower frequency of them mauling each other than I had experienced previously. The leafy greens can be left in pretty large pieces which the little lizards will rip bites off of. Water must be offered in shallow containers to prevent drowning. This generally means the water will need to be replenished a few times daily, as the temperature of the cage will cause rapid evaporation.

Juveniles (four to nine months old)

Once your beardie hits four months old or so, you can relax a little about the size of the prey offered. Insects should still be considerably smaller than the size of the lizard's head, but you needn't be so strict about it. Mealworms can now be offered occasionally, provided they are small enough. To assure that no problems arise from feeding mealworms, feed only those that have just molted; they will be white and soft. They should be large enough to

handle waxworms now, as well. If you want to feed your dragons mice, by this age they should be able to take pinky (hairless, day-old) and maybe fuzzy (furry, week-old) mice. If a given item of food looks too big, it probably is.

Juveniles should be fed daily to twice a day. A handful of crickets should suffice. They are still growing fast at this age but have slowed some from the tremendous rate of a hatchling. Add supplements to the diet every other day, approximately every third or fourth

You owe it to your pet to provide not only excellent housing and diet but also vet care as necessary. Photo by A. Both.

BEARDED DRAGONS

A vet had to amputate the end of this dragon's leg after she was mauled by an aggressive male. Photo by M. Walls.

feeding. Vegetables can be given daily to every other day; if they are still housed in a group it would be best to feed vegetables daily.

Adults (nine months and older)

At this age, very few food items will be too big. Many adult beardies can take large mice without a problem. To be safe, feed prey that is smaller than the lizard's head, and you will never go wrong. Adult bearded dragons, while not growing rapidly, are active, alert lizards. Therefore, they should be fed daily or every other day. Supplements should be given once to twice a week, perhaps a little more to breeding females. Roughly half of the volume of a bearded's diet should be vegetation.

HEALTH

Bearded dragons are very hardy animals, not usually prone to illnesses. There are a few diseases that hobbyists should be aware of, but, with first-rate care, you are unlikely to encounter them. With most reptiles, bearded dragons included, the majority of

health problems are caused by poor husbandry. Therefore, the hobbyist can prevent them by providing excellent housing and diet for his/her animals.

With that in mind, it is important to realize that even well-cared for animals get sick on occasion. Most illness are beyond the capabilities of the average hobbyist to diagnose and treat correctly. If your beardie appears ill, you should seek competent veterinary care immediately. Reptiles rapidly can go from appearing healthy to being dead; do not hesitate to seek care. By competent veterinary care I mean finding a vet who is experienced and trained to care for reptiles. These specialists are slowly becoming easier to find. You can start your search in the phone book, calling vets and pet stores, and asking for recommendations. Make sure the vet you are considering has experience with bearded dragons specifically. Many of these specialists will charge more than a typical vet, but it is well worth the cost.

The symptoms for illnesses vary, obviously. However, there are certain signs that all is not well with your dragon you should be looking for. One of the most important things you can do to recognize failing health in your pet is to observe your dragon daily, learning what is normal in appearance and behavior and what is not. Any changes should be noted and acted upon if needed. Some general symptoms to look for are lack of appetite, sudden weight loss, swelling of any body area, discharge from mouth, eyes, nostrils, or vent, leth-

argy, labored breathing, sunken eyes, and abnormal stools (bloody, runny, smelly, etc.). Symptoms such as these should prompt you to seek emergency care.

Below are some of the most common problems associated with bearded dragons. As stated, beardies are very hardy, so none of these problems is common particularly.

Calcium Deficiency, Metabolic Bone Disease, etc.

Under this heading, I am lumping together a group of different conditions that have similar causes and similar symptoms. All present more or less like rickets in humans, i.e. softening of the bones and skeletal deformities. The cause of these problems is one of three things: too little calcium in the diet, more phosphorus than calcium in the diet, or lack of a source of vitamin D. These conditions are most often seen in hatchlings and juveniles that need tremendous amounts of calcium and vitamin D. These illnesses are easy to prevent by feeding your pet a diet rich in calcium and providing full-spectrum lighting. There are no really good early signs of these conditions. Some things to look for are softening of the jaws, deformities of tail and spine, failure to grow at a normal rate, fractured limbs, swollen and hard limbs, and immobility. In severe cases, there is a total lack of movement, inappetence, and twitching and spasms of the toes, tail, and limbs. Unless the illness goes untreated and has become severe, it is usually reversible by feeding a good diet and providing proper lighting. A vet may

If you need to quarantine your bearded dragon, whether due to illness or his being a new acquisition, keep the cage simple to ease cleaning and disinfecting. Photo by I. Francais.

suggest calcium injections to get your pet back on its feet quickly, and he/she will need to perform x-rays looking for fractures. Hand-feeding or even tube-feeding may be necessary until the jaws firm up a bit.

Injuries, Abscesses, and Burns

Under normal circumstances, these problems are completely preventable. A conscientious keeper will do his/her utmost to keep his/her pet from harm. However, chance and chaos intervene now and then. Bites and other open wounds can be treated easily by the keeper if they are very minor. Direct pressure will stop bleeding, and wounds can be cleaned with water and some antiseptic. Keep it clean and dab it with some triple antibiotic ointment several times daily. If the wound is deep, keeps

bleeding, or shows any signs of infection, see a vet as soon as possible. Most wounds are preventable by keeping sharp decorations out of the enclosure, handling your beardie only in a secure area, and keeping beardies away from other pets. Beardies sometimes bite each other severely. In that case, further traumas can be prevented by separating the combatants.

Abscesses are formed from small, untreated wounds. The wounds become infected and a lump of pus forms. Abscesses are serious because they represent a reservoir of bacteria and toxins within the body. Left untreated, they will eventually rupture and septicemia will result. Abscesses require veterinary treatment. The vet will open, clean, drain, and suture the abscess while also prescribing

antibiotics to combat further infection.

Burns generally occur when a reptile is allow to get too close to a heating lamp. They also occur when heating devices malfunction. Always be sure a dragon cannot come in contact with bulbs and emitters. Check your heaters frequently with a thermometer to be sure the temperature they create is not too hot or too cold. If you are using a thermostat to control lights and other heat sources, having a back-up will save your animals if the primary one fails. Most burns will require veterinary care immediately, as burns are frequently accompanied by shock and dehydration.

Mites

These nasty creepy-crawlies are the bane of all lizard and snake keepers. They are tiny

BEARDED DRAGONS

relatives of ticks that feed off the blood of reptiles. Once established in a collection, they are very difficult to get rid of. They will lay eggs in the terrarium and expand their population rapidly. The spiny scales of bearded dragons provide ample places for mites to hide. Besides the energy drain they cause, mites also can carry bacteria and cause infections.

Mites can be hard to see. They resemble little blackish dots wandering around on your animal. Often they are first noticed drowned in the water bowl. Their feces are a whitish powder that can be more noticeable than the mites themselves.

There are many treatments for mites available. Many rely on highly toxic agents that can adversely affect the dragons. These include the pest strips so many hobbyist swear by. Vets usually prescribe ivermectin in a spray to mist the cage and animals. This is usually very safe (never use it on turtles as it will cause them neurological damage). Pet stores also carry many mite products of varying effectiveness.

A very safe mite remedy is regular cooking oil. You can use olive, vegetable, or corn oil. Immerse the beardie in the oil, being sure to wet the corners of the jaws, the eyelids, the vent, and the nostrils. Blot him dry and leave him in a sterile enclosure for a day or two. If this is a new animal that has mites, you can now move him to his permanent enclosure. If this is a beardie you have owned for a while, you will need to destroy the mites in his enclosure. The cage and all the fixtures must be soaked in a strong solution of bleach and water. The longer they soak the better, but a half hour is normally sufficient. Be sure to rinse them thoroughly to remove all traces of bleach; bleach fumes cause respiratory problems and may contribute to the development of cancer. The bedding should be thrown away and replaced. Now, you can move the beardie into a clean, mite-free home. The oil treatment usually will cause the animal to go into shedding soon afterward. This is normal.

Next to its owner, a veterinarian with a reptile specialty is a bearded dragon's best friend. It is best to find a reptile vet before emergencies arise. Photo by J. Balzarini.

Growing a hatchling into a beautiful, healthy adult like this one requires paying careful attention to their diet and other needs. Photo by I. Francais.

HANDLING and TRAINING

To most hobbyists keeping bearded dragons, the primary reason to keep them is their delightful personality. Although a few are aggressive, the vast majority are friendly and seem to enjoy some interaction and handling. With only some slight effort on the keeper's part, his or her bearded dragon will become "dog tame."

HANDLING

Bearded dragons are not delicate, so handling them doesn't present any major problems. Always keep in mind the size of these animals. Handle them with some care, as they are far smaller than you. They will not appreciate any roughhousing, and they do not play. These are not puppies and will not form familial attachments with their keepers. Among other things, this means that if they feel overly threatened by careless handling, they will bite. Although unpleasant, bloody, and painful, bites from bearded dragons are not serious. Because all reptiles carry a variety of bacteria, protozoa, and other microscopic nasties in their mouths, clean all bite wounds with some form of antiseptic and keep an eye out for signs of infection.

With these cautions in mind, handling your beardie should be fun and stress-free. Before taking your dragon out of its lair, be sure you are in a secure area free of commotion and hazards. Lots of people milling about, loud noises, etc. may startle your beardie into bolting. Granted, most are very relaxed once they get used to being handled, but none of them are above being

Hatchling beardies must be handled gently. It is easy to injure these tiny creatures if you are careless in picking them up. Photo by I. Francais.

For the most part, bearded dragons are remarkably tolerant of handling. More than almost any other lizard, they truly are deserving of the term "pet." Photo by I. Francais.

scared or startled. Be careful of other pets. Cats in particular will take a great interest in the handling routine. If you get distracted, your cute little lizard could become lunch for your dog, cat, or ferret.

I'll start by assuming your beardie is a nice one; I'll discuss aggressive ones later. The best way to pick one up is to sort of scoop it up under the body with your palm. Try to support as much of the body as possible and give the legs some support. If the legs are left dangling, the lizard will be uncomfortable and may flail around. Move smoothly and with confidence. Jerky motions can frighten the animal. Once you have the animal elevated, you can

place it on your shoulder, if you like. Be prepared for it to jump, but most of the time most beardies will perch contentedly. A few of mine are calm enough that I can walk around doing minor housework with them sitting still on my shoulder. Not all are this trusting, so you will need to get to know your particular beardie.

Much of what I've written above applies to adults and to good-sized juveniles. Hatchlings will need to be handled with considerably more caution. Scoop them up in your hand gently, careful not to squish them. Hatchlings are normally more flighty than the adults, so be prepared for them to dash away at the slightest distur-

bance. Although they are usually not hurt by falling, the chance always exists that they will break a bone or cause some internal damage to themselves. It is best to allow them to rest in one hand, shielding them from disturbance with the other. As with the adults, some are calmer than others. Frequently handling a hatchling will help ensure it grows into a docile adult.

TAMING

Taming an irascible bearded dragon is a different experience from handling an adult. An aggressive hatchling poses no danger other than some painful pinching. However, a well-fed baby will quickly grow to a size enabling them to draw blood. It is wise to tame your dragon down before it gets to that point.

The best way to tame a beardie is to refuse to be intimidated; handle it briefly everyday despite all the threats. Grab the lizard swiftly but gently around the body, avoiding the mouth, of course. Once in hand hold it firmly, and when it calms down, stroke its head. The key here is persistence. Some of the nasty beardies will tame in a couple of weeks and others will take months. Keep at it. Eventually, your trouble will pay off. You can also hand feed your dragon while holding it (being careful not to get bitten in the process). This way it may begin to associate handling with a treat. Some beardies may be untamable, but these are very few and far between. Continue your taming efforts for several months before giving up. It is probably best not to breed

Even unruly bearded dragons calm down usually. Be patient and don't be intimidated by their bluffing. Photo by I. Francais.

You should support as much of your dragon's weight as possible when holding him. If he feels insecure, he may jump or flail around. Photo by I. Francais.

BEARDED DRAGONS

these pugnacious animals, on the off chance that aggressiveness is an inheritable trait.

HYGIENE

Almost every animal, including human beings, carries with it a host of microorganisms of various types. Most of these organisms cause no harm, and some are even beneficial. An example from the human digestive tract is *E. coli*, a species of bacteria. *E. coli* lives in the human large intestine making vitamin K as part of its metabolism, which humans then utilize. Some of these organisms can cause illness when introduced to another host or to an area of their usual host

where they do not normally occur. Thus, *E. coli* can cause an infection if it enters the human eye or an open wound.

Getting back to bearded dragons, like other animals, they carry around a plethora of microorganisms normally. When you handle your dragon and its cage fixtures, some of these microbes are transferred to the skin of your hands. If you put your fingers in your mouth or rub your eyes, you can become infected with one or more of these microbes. Most of the time, the infections are not serious; they will cause some diarrhea, cramps, and/or vomiting. However, these infections are especially dangerous to

children, the elderly, and those with compromised immune systems. Preventing these infections is not difficult. Wash your hands immediately after every handling session and every time you touch cage fixtures. Never allow a reptile access to any food-preparation areas. Never eat or drink while cleaning the cage or handling the animal. If you use a sink or bathtub to clean cages or bathe your reptiles, rinse it out with a strong bleach solution. If you follow these procedures, you probably will never contract an illness from your reptile. In all my years of keeping herps, I've never had an illness that I could attribute to my pets.

Like many other reptiles, cats, dogs, and birds, bearded dragons can carry pathogenic bacteria. Always wash your hands after handling your beardie or any of her cage furnishings. Photo by I. Francais.

BREEDING

In modern herpetoculture, the prevailing attitude seems to be that breeding a species is the only possible reason for keeping the species in the first place. While this might be true for some people, it certainly is not true for a large segment of the hobby. Also, certain herps are produced in such huge numbers on a commercial scale, there seems to be an overpopulation problem. It's becoming hard to find homes for all the Corn Snakes, Burmese Pythons, and Leopard Geckos being bred by hobbyists. The same is true of Inland Bearded Dragons. The other species of bearded dragons are still uncommon in the hobby.

Bearded dragons are a prolific and easily bred species. The eggs have a high rate of hatching, and most of the hatchlings survive. Only a few years ago, bearded dragons fetched high prices, further encouraging hobbyists to breed them. Now, they are so abundant on the pet market that the prices have fallen dramatically, and homes for the babies are getting harder to find in some areas. This issue must be addressed before a hobbyist decides to go ahead and breed

his or her dragons. Make sure you know you can find good homes for the offspring or be willing to keep them. Remember that bearded dragons are unlikely to make you rich.

Keeping this in mind, it cannot be ignored that breeding a species is fun, educating, and fulfilling. No matter how easy to breed a species is

Bearded dragons are very prolific. Here are several clutches incubating on vermiculite. Photo by I. Francais.

supposed to be, breeding it always feels like an accomplishment. Even beyond any economic reasons, it is easy to understand why hobbyists breed their animals. And, baby dragons are so darn cute!

GUYS AND DOLLS

Telling male bearded dragons from female bearded dragons is not very difficult if you have adults. The hatchlings and juveniles are

harder to tell apart. In the adults you should be able to see the femoral pores of the males. These are small pores located on the underside of the thighs and sometimes just above the vent. These pores are used by the males to mark their territories. Females may have pores, but they will be tiny if not invisible.

The tails of males tend to be swollen at the base immediately following the vent. These swellings are called hemipenile bulges. The hemipenes are the copulatory organs of the males. There is a pair of them, one lying on either side of the vent, in a kind of inside-out configuration. When the male is aroused and ready to mate, the hemipenes fold outward and engorge with blood. It is the presence of the hemipenes that causes the bulges, hence, the females do not have them.

Generally, males grow larger then the females and are built much more stockily. They can be up to 6 inches longer than a female, but usually the difference is not quite so great. The heads of males are proportionally larger and blocky when compared to those of the females.

Vent area of a breeding male. Note the enlarged pores on the underside of the thighs. Some males also have enlarged scales in front of the vent. Photo by M. Walls.

Lastly, behavior often provides excellent clues to the sex of a bearded dragon. Males are territorial and will go through territorial displays periodically, even if housed by themselves with no dragons nearby to display to. These displays are series of vigorous head-bobbing. Males often will inflate their black beards as part of this display or when they feel threatened. The females rarely engage in this type of territoriality (but they do occasionally), and they do not inflate their beards readily. When they do inflate their beards, they are not usually the jet black color of the males'. When they feel threatened, females often engage in the curious arm-waving behavior. Although submissive males also will do this, the dominant male in a group will not.

Juveniles and hatchlings are harder to sex, as the secondary sexual characteristics have not yet developed. With the hatchlings, you sometimes can "pop" the hemipenes of the males. This entails putting gentle pressure to the base of the tail. If done correctly, the hemipenes of the male will "pop" out. Obviously with females, there is nothing to pop out. This can lead to someone wondering if the animal is female or if they just are not pressing hard enough. Popping is a delicate procedure, and it is very possible to injure the animal while performing it. **Definitely** have an experienced person show you how to do this.

Vent area of a breeding female. The pores along the thighs are much smaller than those on the males. Photo by M. Walls.

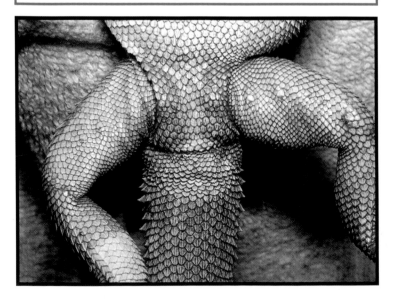

SETTING THE MOOD

It is often stated in the hobby literature that a keeper must vary the keeping conditions in order to get bearded dragons to breed. However, it has been my experience that I need to do nothing other than keep my dragons in excellent condition, and they will breed more often than I want them to. I suspect that bearded dragons have been captive-bred over enough generations that they have adapted to the constant conditions of the terrarium. Interestingly, I have had breeding activity in the winter and summer but never in the fall and only once in the spring. So, it is perfectly possible that the dragons are reacting to seasonal variations in conditions that are too subtle for a lowly human like myself to pick up on.

The other bearded dragons in the hobby, namely the Coastal Bearded Dragon and Rankin's Dragon, may need a little more work to breed than the Inland Bearded Dragon. There is a strong possibility that individuals will breed without any overt manipulation of the keeping conditions, but it is more likely that the keeper will need to cycle these species. There also are individual Inland Bearded Dragons that need cycling in order to come into reproductive condition. I also have heard from some hobbyists that Rankin's Dragon exhibits very low fertility in the terrarium. This may be from inbreeding due to a very limited gene pool.

Although the concept of cycling may frighten some keepers, it is not too difficult to execute. It is helpful to know the natural reasons cycling works in the terrarium. Most animals (though far from all) are seasonal breeders. They time their reproductive efforts so that the young are born at the time conditions are best for their survival. In most cases this translates to the spring or summer. It would be maladaptive in most cases to have vulnerable young emerging when the weather is harsh and food is scarce. At these times, many reptiles retire to shelters and become torpid. This torpidity varies in degree and length, not only by the species of reptile, but also by the severity of the conditions in the habitat. Individuals of

Judging by the shape and size of this dragon's head, it is probably female. Males' heads are proportionally larger and more hefty in appearance. Photo by I. Francais.

one species in one area may be more or less completely dormant for a few months, while those in an area with milder winters may only take shelter during the harshest weather, and all variations in between may exist. Over most of the area that bearded dragons are found, the winters are mild enough to allow some activity during this season.

When the conditions again become favorable, the lizards emerge and become active. This dormancy followed by activity and food intake

Male bearded dragons tend to have wide heads. The beard of the male also is more well developed than that of the female. Photo by M. Walls.

BEARDED DRAGONS

stimulates the endocrine and reproductive systems. The males produce sperm, and the females ovulate. The lizards mate and produce young. The young are born or hatch early enough in the season to grow and gain weight to survive the winter and start the cycle again.

Obviously that is a simplified account of the seasonal activity of many lizards. The purpose is to give you an idea of what may stimulate your beardies to reproduce. You do not have to provide severe winter weather; you just need to provide a sense of seasonal rhythms.

Perhaps the two most important factors to control are temperature and photoperiod. It also seems that food

intake is important, but this is affected by the other two. In normal keeping conditions, summer as it were, the temperatures in the terrarium are in the 80's and 90's, and there are 12 to 15 hours of light each day. You will need to change the conditions to reflect a mild winter for a few weeks. These changes should be done gradually; in nature summer does not change to winter in 24 hours. At their lowest, temperatures nearest the basking lights should be no more than 80 to 83°F (26 to 29°C) with temperatures significantly lower in other areas of the terrarium. At night, the temperatures may safely drop into the upper 50's, but there is no need to drop them below 65°F (18°C).

You will want to gradually change the photoperiod so that the dragons only receive 9 to 11 hours of light each day. The lowest temperatures should coincide with the shortest daylengths. Make sure there is some sort of retreat available to the dragons or a deep enough substrate for them to burrow into.

During the artificial winter, the dragons will decrease their food intake and may stop eating entirely. The decreased temperatures will slow down the rate of their digestion. So, you should cut back their feedings to only twice a week, less if they seem to not be eating when you feed them. Keep supplementing the diet with vitamins and minerals roughly every fourth

Hybrids between the Inland Bearded Dragon and Rankin's Dragon sometimes are produced by breeders. In some cases, these young are infertile. Photo by R. D. Bartlett.

Here is a female digging a nest in moist sand. It is important to the health of the female and the eggs that you provide her with a proper nesting site. Photo by I. Francais.

BEARDED DRAGONS

In most of the color phases of bearded dragons, the male shows the color better than the female. Photo by G. Merker and W. Merker.

BEARDED DRAGONS

Remove the eggs from the nest carefully, avoiding any turning or jarring. Photo by I. Francais.

feeding. Keep offering food, even if they only eat sporadically or not at all. Of course, clean water must be available at all times.

After 8 to 12 weeks of winter, begin to bring the temperatures and photoperiod back up to normal levels. The change should be made at about the same rate as the change to winter conditions. Once the conditions are back to normal, begin feeding the breeders heavily. You should be giving the female an additional serving of vitamin and mineral supplements weekly. This will provide her with the calcium and other vitamins and minerals necessary to produce eggs. Fuzzy and hopper mice, which are rich in fat and calcium, are good for keeping the energy and mineral reserves of breeding females high.

Submersible aquarium heaters can be used to keep a homemade incubator the proper temperature. Keep the heater totally submerged, or it will malfunction. Photo by M. Walls.

CONJUGAL RELATIONS

If you are housing your males and females separately, now is the time to put them together. Males will engage in serious territorial displays, bobbing heads and inflating beards. Females may join in as well and may engage in submissive arm-waving if the males are ready to breed before they are.

As with many lizards, the mating behavior of bearded dragons is rough. The male grasps the nape of the female in his jaws without any ceremony. Sometimes the male will drag the female around the cage a little before actually copulating. Eventu-

Commercial chicken incubators can be adapted for use with bearded dragon eggs. Photo by I. Francais.

ally, the male will wrap his tail under the female's to bring their vents together. He will erect his hemipenes and insert one into the female's vent. Copulation is usually brief, lasting no more than a minute or two, if that. Bearded dragons generally will copulate many times over the course of the day.

It is common for the male to leave bite marks on the neck of the female. This normally is no cause for alarm. However, occasionally males will get very aggressive with the females. They can cause the females serious damage, even death. Breeding females sometimes lose feet and tails to the aggressive males. If you see any evidence the male is attacking the female, they must be separated. Having a large enclosure and keeping multiple females housed with a single male will help prevent such aggression.

MOTHERHOOD

A month or so after mating, the female will start to take on a swollen look. This is due to the production of eggs. As she gets closer to laying, she will only get larger. During this time, you must keep the female on an excellent diet if you want her to produce healthy babies and remain healthy herself. Give her extra food and vitamins. She will probably stop eating right before laying the eggs.

Once it becomes obvious your female is gravid, you will need to give her a place to lay her eggs. Females not provided with an adequate nesting site may scatter their eggs over the substrate or even lay them in the water bowl. In either case, it is not likely the offspring will survive. It is even more likely the female will retain the eggs in her oviducts, a condition called egg-binding. This is a very serious condition. If the eggs are retained for a significant amount of time, the young will die and the eggs become increasingly calcified. Eventually, this causes the oviduct tissue to die and necrotize. At this point, the female is gravely ill and in desperate need of veterinary attention. Far better to have given her a suitable nesting site in the beginning.

If fed heavily and given space, baby beardies can be kept together without problems. Be sure to separate any that are picked on by their siblings. Photo by M. Walls.

Truth be told, females are not terribly fussy about where they lay their eggs. Therefore, a nest box is rather easy to construct. Medium- to large-sized cat litter pans suffice as the box. There are quite a few media that you can use in the box, including sand, vermiculite, potting soil, and cactus soil. I prefer vermiculite because it is lightweight and very absorbent, but any of the materials mentioned will work fine. Fill the box near to the top. Add enough water to make the material moist but not soggy. The female should dig in the box without need of encouragement, but sometimes making a shallow depression will attract her interest.

Usually the female will dig several different holes in the box. She may spend several days doing nothing but digging. Eventually, she will dig a deep hole, settle in, and lay her eggs. Eggs are generally laid in the afternoon. If you are housing your bearded dragons outside, it is wise to mark the site of egg deposition. When a female is done

The siblings of this bearded dragon nipped off his toes as a hatchling. Feed the babies well to avoid this. Photo by M. Walls.

BEARDED DRAGONS

Selective breeding has begun to produce some particularly attractive beardies. This is a gold phase male. Photo by R. Hunziker.

laying her eggs she will cover the nest well enough to make it almost invisible. Normal clutches contain 12 to 24 eggs, sometimes fewer or more. Young females and old females generally lay smaller clutches. There are roughly three or four years of peak reproductive performance, after which egg production declines sharply.

Once the eggs are laid, you will need to dig them up and

This dragon sports a fire-toned beard and makes a desirable breeder. Photo by M. Walls.

move them into an incubator for the best hatching results. Dig up the eggs carefully. I have found that a tablespoon makes a good tool for unearthing eggs in the nesting box. Try your best not to turn or jar the eggs as you transfer them as this can kill the embryos. If the eggs are stuck together, leave them that way. You are likely to break them if you try to separate them.

PROPERLY "COOKING" THE EGGS

It is best to have an incubator up and running before you need it. This allows you to have the temperature and humidity at the proper levels and gives you a chance to fix any problems before the incubator is full of delicate eggs. You can either buy an incubator or make one. Most pet stores do not carry incubators, but some do. Incubators for chicken eggs will work well and can be found at many farm and garden stores. You will need to add a pan of water to these incubators to bring the humidity up to an accept-

able level. With the booming interest in herpetoculture which has occurred in the last several years has come a proliferation of companies that sell a wide range of herp-specific products, including incubators. Check for these companies in a herp magazine or at your nearest herp expo.

It is quite simple to make your own incubator. There are a number of materials that you can use to build an incubator; one of the most satisfactory is a polystyrene box, like those used to ship tropical fish. Most pet stores are happy to give these boxes away, especially if you are a regular customer. You must be certain the box you use does not leak, or you will end up with water all over your floor and desiccated eggs. Place two bricks in the bottom of the box. These will keep the egg container above the water. Add water until it is just short of covering the bricks. A 25-watt submersible aquarium heater will serve to keep the proper temperature, and a thermometer will allow you to keep track of it. I highly recommend digital thermometers with external probes and the capability of storing the maximum and minimum temperatures. This allows you to check the temperature without opening the incubator and to know the range of temperatures maintained. You will probably have to fuss with the heater to keep the range of temperatures tolerable. You should have the incubator set up and maintaining the proper temperature for at least 48 hours prior to placing the eggs inside. Bearded dragon eggs are reasonably

Hatchling beardies of most of the colorful forms show very little beyond typical coloration. This female red phased hatchling is just beginning to show some color. Photo by K. H. Switak.

hardy, but they will do best when incubated at 85°F (29°C). A little cooler will cause no harm other than a longer incubation period, but temperatures in excess of 88°F (31°C) likely will cause birth defects and death.

The only thing you need to add to the above is a container of incubation medium to place the eggs in. Plastic food storage containers will work well, as will a number of other similar things. Poke many holes in the lid to provide ventilation. Alternatively, you can skip the lid until the eggs are close to hatching. Several times I have had hatchlings climb out of the container and fall in the water without harm (they generally

climb up the sides of the incubator and cling there).

Most breeders use vermiculite as the incubation medium. It holds humidity very well while allowing air to circulate around the eggs. Additionally it does not harbor bacteria or mold. Fill the container with vermiculite, remembering to leave room for the water and the hatchlings. Add water and mix thoroughly. The vermiculite should be damp but not soggy. A good test is to squeeze a little bit between your fingers. A drop or two of water should drip off but not more than that. A little drier than that will probably cause no harm since the water in the bottom will keep the relative humidity high.

Transfer the eggs to the incubation medium without turning them. They should be about two-thirds buried in the vermiculite. If possible, the eggs should not be touching each other or the sides of the container. Check them frequently, at least twice a week. Eggs that are fungused, collapsed, or seriously leaking should be discarded. You also will have to keep an eye on the water level. If the aquarium heater sticks up above the water surface it could malfunction or crack, creating a serious fire hazard.

Under the incubation conditions described, bearded dragon eggs will take from 50 to 70 days to hatch. Around this time, you must begin to

BEARDED DRAGONS

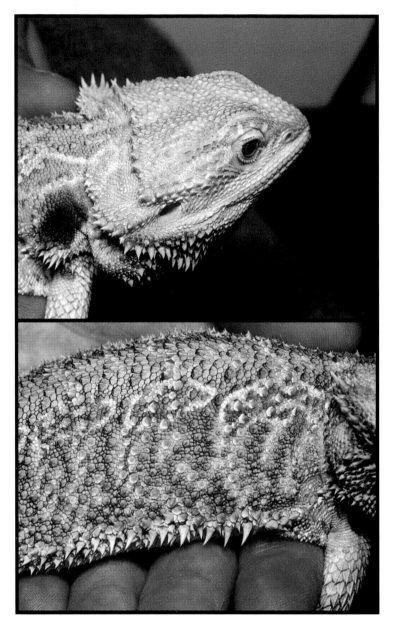

Head and body views of a colorful bearded dragon owned by the author. This male approaches being a tiger phase dragon, but he is a little light in color and the ocelli are less distinct than in a true tiger. Photos by M. Walls.

water bowl is not deep enough for the babies to drown in. A few bottle caps will work. You should mist the hatchlings with a plant sprayer for the first few days, as they probably will not eat or drink. Once they are eating, you can discontinue spraying them.

It is best to house hatchling bearded dragons by themselves. However, given the large numbers of young a female can produce, this usually is not possible. A compromise would be to break them up into groups by size, keeping only similarly sized young together. This will keep competition for food at a minimum. Once they start eating, you should feed them well and often. Otherwise, they will begin to pick on each other, and soon you will have hatchlings with missing tails, toes, and feet. Keeping some edible fruits and vegetables available all of the time seriously will reduce the amount of aggression between your babies. Refer to the chapter on feeding for more specific guidelines.

check on them daily. It is best to move the hatchlings from the incubator to the cage as soon as possible, but do not rush them. Let them come out of the egg on their own. It has been my experience that bearded dragons do not need any assistance to hatch. Some may take longer than others, but this is normal. The vast majority of the eggs will hatch within a day of each other.

RAISING DRAGONS

As with the incubator, it is best to have housing ready and waiting for the babies instead of having to cobble it together at the last minute. For the most part, the hatchlings can be housed in the same conditions as the adults. The cage fixtures will need to be appropriately sized for the tiny lizards. In particular, you should make sure the

VARIATIONS ON A THEME

With the large numbers of bearded dragons being bred, it was inevitable that color and pattern variations would become established. There are currently several that are available to the hobbyist, most costing substantially more than a normally colored individual. It is wise to look at

Well-marked red phased dragons such as this one are attractive animals. They often are priced according to how red the parents are, with the reddest ones being the most expensive. Photo by G. & C. Merker.

the parents of any of these designer hatchlings, since in many the color is poorly distinguished. Looking at the parents will give you a good idea how distinct the hatchlings may end up being, as most hatchlings look very similar.

Red

This is the most common of the designer dragons. In well-colored individuals, the head is a dark orangey-red with a deep reddish wash to the rest of the body. The dorsal ocelli may be particularly orange or red with the spaces in between them being a sort of grayish, brownish purple. The males show the color best, but the females are quite attractive. Too often the animals sold as red-phase

dragons have only the barest hint of red to them.

Gold

This form frequently is barely distinct from normal bearded dragons. Generally, the animals are pale with a light wash of yellow to the head and dorsum. Well-colored specimens are very pretty. They are a light, mustardy to sunny yellow over most of the head and back. The dorsal ocelli may be gray to a nearly purple color. There is a similar morph called "gold head" that retains the normal bearded dragon coloration except on the head, which is mustardy yellow.

Tiger

The tiger phase is a re-cently developed morph that

is quite beautiful when fully developed. A good tiger bearded has rich, red-brown ocelli with black bars in between them. The overall color is similar to that of the red phase, but the red is not so apparent. There is great variation in the development of the pattern, and the hobbyist is warned to view the parents before purchasing a hatchling.

Snow

This is the newest morph of which I am aware. It is very rare in the hobby; I have only seen one photograph of one. The animal was pale white with the pattern still visible but subdued. The eyes were normally colored, so this is not a form of albinism. Only time will tell if this form will become established.

BEARDED DRAGONS

Bearded dragons when well cared for live for 7 to 12 years. You must be committed to care for that hatchling for its entire lifespan before you purchase it. Photo by G. & C. Merker.